Balance Sheet

Balance Sheet

Kit Robinson

ROOF BOOKS
New York

ISBN: 0-937804-52-5
Library of Congress Catalog Card No.: 93-085180

Parts of this book have appeared in *Five Fingers Review, O/2: an anthology, o•blek, The Bay Guardian, SHINY, Mirage#4/Period(ical), Avec, Long News: In the Short Century, LetterBox,* and *lower limit speech.*

Counter Meditation appeared as a chapbook from Zasterle Press in Tenerife, Spain, 1991.

Cover by Bill Luoma.
Book design by Deborah Thomas.
Author photo by Ericka McConnell.

This book was made possible, in part, by a grant from the New York State Council on the Arts.

Roof Books
are published by
Segue Foundation
303 East 8th Street
New York, New York 10009

To James Keith Robinson

July 24, 1916–January 4, 1993

Table of Contents

Counter Meditation

1

Slow down
and the insects catch up with you.
Slow down even more
and they fly right past you
mistaking you for a wooden stump.

2

An insect writing
would appear immobile
to a human.

An insect writing
to a human
would appear immobile.

A human writing
would appear immobile
to an insect.

A human writing
to a human
would not appear.

3

Two people kiss,
go off together.

What happens next
is on them.

4

When a city looks at a person
it sees only the sky.
Rivers flow through the city,
light consumes them.

5

One size fits all —
the ring
the wheel
the stash . . .

Hanging out
on the periphery
of occupation

I sounded it out
to hammer sounds
in leaf shade

moving with the wind.
A man was working
on an addition.

Vapor trail
like a giant eyebrow
over clouds, houses,
trees, ditch, fence,
and picnic table top —
fans out
into light blue.

6

Between a rock
and a soft spot
unity
and virtual fragmentation

the United States Postal Service
Commemorative Stamp Club
makes its presence felt
on the eclectic American plain.

7

If all words
were blown away,
which words
would be the first
to recur?

Does what's said
grow like a sprout
from silent earth?
Or is it a belt
in a moving assembly
of words?

"yes"
"hot"
"way"

Slowly at first
building a house to last
corners cut
in the ongoing course of events

the way I figure
and the way interruptions collide
the body turns over
sleep startles the owner
in time to wake with all things.

8

You have completely mastered everything.

Now what!?

9

Our life is composed
of fragments
stitched in sleep.

Days weave the light
skin tight against the thought
of which our life is composed.

10

I got one of your moons today.
The space behind it whitened and went out.

These words occurred to me
somewhere in Helsinki.
They seemed to come from you.

I showed them to you
and you said you might take them back,
to which I agreed, absentmindedly.

11

What is an hour?
Clothespin.

A black dog
sticking its head
out an open window,
fruit trees turning yellow.

Then it is gone,
the window closed shut,
the house yellow.

Sun on my back.
"That incredible piece of crap"
overheard in an instant.

Sometimes you just have to wait it out.
In any case it will up.

A dreamy lake or crowded bus?
Statuary.

12

Lawyerly, consumable, forego,
questioning, axiomatic, ripen,
desist, topiary, preclude.

What is it
of a Sunday afternoon
curls the insides
of the weak?

The week:
Inexorable, exoskeletal, cross-hatched,
pejorative, compulsory, clenched
province of restless, hungry ghosts!

Riding the gain
to prevent feedback,
stealing a page
from every little package,
increasing the hit rate
through reducing our store count,
"What business are we in?"
Reswizzling the mix.

13

Off the self.
Objects, realms. Water
runs north-south.

Work is percussion.
Belief. The lines
get tangled up.

Breath is right,
making a transitive
verb of light.

14

The stars have spaces around them.
Go ahead, Ron,
write that down.

In a spirited attack
on bourgeois conventions
the avant-garde breathes life
into the exhaust, hovering
over the neighborhood
mostly working class
of the Piazza Santo Spirito.

But we, conversely,
are beginning our gradual descent
into Salt Lake City.

15

And not rake leaves
or not to call a friend
the things I am not doing
support me

in this
my upper body wonder
placed at a mat in fall.

16

I've been in Jimmy & Lucy's House of K,
and I've read in the Red Hall,
and now here I am
on Sol Uhuru's Art Shack.

But wherever I am
I'm not entirely there
because I have to leave room
for this.

17

When in society
the conversation faltered
and silence threatened
to become oppressive

the Russian people
used to say,
"Durak rodilsa!" "The
Fool is born!"

Welcome to the
world, old son.

(Today, says Alyosha,
they would say
something less polite.)

18

The form of all lands
is formlessness — in all worlds
there only exists verbal expression,
and verbal expression has no basis in facts.
Furthermore, facts have no basis in words.
All worlds are silent.
All the teachings add nothing.

Names, rounds, Americans,
citizens, troops, taxes, makers,
lawyers, headlines, concepts,
years, reports, votes, companies,
prices, users, concerns, bankruptcies —
the nature of all phenomena is uncreated.

The open doorway
of a plain brick building front
through which the interior walls
have poured down the stairs
and out into a huge pile
of rubble on the street.

A photograph of the sun.

19

Eve off.
As in, "We get Christmas Eve off."

20

Nothing compares to the impermanence of this
(a) bright fall day
(b) convenience store model
(c) imaginary voice
(d) thought: "Nothing compares to this . . ." etc.

We ride the rails of history, fending
with the best of them,
letters to what's left of us
from writers to the west of us
changing modalities
in time to the weather.

That's easy for you to say.

Imagine every instant as an initial.
Imagine an intimate opera as all of an instant.

It was over before it began.
It took forever.

21

The limitations of
a brown notebook
are three inches

by five inches
by a person
unable to escape

from a shadow
of fluctuating dimensions
even in a hundred thousand million eternities.

22

It all went down
and it went well —
the fantasy,
the concept,
the meditation,
the business about the truck . . .

It all came down
to the body. The body
was in bad shape.

Rest.
Time will ship the darts and larks.

23

That one knows and is
only desire
deconstructs the problem
of being a person

so that the elements
of living are laid out
across a plane transversed
by waking solids —

no negatives
no bleeds
no color
no discounts for multiples.

24

Delusions are inexhaustible.
I vow to enter them!

The huge sand-strewn esplanade
The mostly empty parking lot
A few flakes of snow . . .

While you were out
some vague details
ate your lunch.

25

I like the specificity of the word "vague."
The incisive initial "v" cuts through the mind
like a stylus riding a groove.
The silent "u" lies in wait
to snare the hurried, unwary reader.
In French it means "wave"
and by its Latin root
it's related to "vagrant" and "vagabond"
though not to "vagina," which comes
from the word for "sheath."
By calling something "vague,"
I advance a standard of accuracy, a belief
in the possibility of definition,
an optimism brimming with purchase.
I have a vague notion
and stepping toward the light
I enter the world's care.

26

If tomorrow the headlines
are three inches high
it means how many
thousands will die?

A sad mathematics
counts the ways
men of greed
have corrupted our days.

Dear President Bush,
Please read our sighs.
Prove your love
not your penis size.

This song is old
but the meaning is clear:
Bring our troops home.
Stop the war!

27

I love you, automaton!
I love you, work machine!
I love you, production unit!

Take an aspirin!
Have a good day at work!

28

There is nothing
to write about.

Rain once
in a long while,
intense assignment
followed by free fall,
the personal dissolve.

When you close the book
the wet ink prints
backwards
on the opposite page
a desiccated Semitic script
illegible by half.

When you wander through
those ruins stand
for whatever you pick up
on the back of your mind
pressed against doorways
whose walls are no longer
leaning in
under a steady barrage of dead signs.

The night sky
is terrible.
Periods
can't be distinguished
from noise.

29

The yellow ribbon
tied to a tree
my country
'tis of thee.

What do you mean, guy?
Why don't you say?
I can't, I'm thousands
of miles away

fighting a war
that can't be won
and to think my life
had just begun

while on the home front
poverty
is carpet-bombing
my family.

These words flashed on
no LED
but occurred almost
transparently

amid commuters'
pale distraction —
under the breath
they sense death.

30

A sense of honor
propels him
frames the man
in his young body

not to abandon
his buddies
not to let them down.
The rest

is unknowable really
except as noble words
that get lost
in a high wind.

When I was, I was
and when I wasn't
I wasn't going to stick around
to find out.

31

Look for discrepancies in your totem pole.

32

How could you want to write
something one time
and not want to write
it another?

Time circles the missing term.
It's on the map. As a matter
of fact, so are we. The subject
changed. Why not go

back and recover some
of the same ground?
"You are always burning
your bridges."

Yes, because there's
only so much:
no danger of falling
over the edge of the world.

33

The day the war
ended it started
to rain. It rained
for four days, as if
in expression of grief.

America felt
better about itself, we
were told. The dead spoke
and were more eloquent.

The specter of Viet Nam
was not vanquished
but remained on our streets
in the person of persons
deprived of adequate shelter.
The rain soaked them.

34

Luck hoisted us
into second place.
The air was
on. The money

would be in
the mail. A
fine mist fell
across the freeway

all night, as
we slept in
houses and were
smug as clams.

We had done
fairly well in
the betting pool.

35

Make-up, athleticism, style:
all shields we
hold up to
block the inevitable

sun, death,
you tell us,
my dear doctor-at-arms,

and no way
have we pulled
down our vanity

but we wear
it lightly, because
art is nothing

but consummate artfulness
in all things:
no capital A
but a lower

case study in
going along, coming
soon to a
theater near you.

36

My taste is dragged
by others' wits
past half cancellation.
Doubt, tits, face, and aspirin laugh.
I feel left out.
When is a man
a flotation device?
When up in the air
or at sea?
I'll call you later.

37

Dear Manuel Brito,
Again the money
is certainly a

true statement of
the way things
are here too.

38

Why this obsessive need
to record? Why this
going back over? This
reduction of transient, ephemeral
lived experience to marks
on page, tape, or
disk to be pored
over from every imaginable
angle later? Repeatedly?

"Once you hear the
music, it's gone in
the air . . . you can
never capture it again."

November 1990–April 1991

Balance Sheet

Pieced lines and lined pieces lead to the blind shed, its light
green finish peeled off before the eyes can catch hold. Stasis
has become a way to get the job done, an unlikely reminder
blessed with the virtues inherent in a peach pit, part of something
much longer, but remaining, for the time being, a cradle to stillness.

Falling then into an imitation of sleep, the western writer
dreams of spurs, cactus, and Comanche trails still fresh
in his imagination, he being a man of no small ends and
having a surplus bond with nature. It seems so simple
that even a foreign parliament could vote on it without translating

its parameters into an equivalent juvenile stream, the worst
of it being over, the first a quick glance to the left
of center. Progress seals its own fate when getting down with
a debenture or two, and the only way around it is to fake
a rhythm into the rectilinear booster for half an age.

Then the ornamental report falls due. A mix angles into view
while cherry blossoms come down on either side, and the nether
world coughs jargon up into the fan. The history lesson
collapses into giggles, because there really isn't any way
of determining what led to this impasse, only an alignment

tending to grace the weather, a particle haven, a spit
on which to roast the occasion, for all the good it will do.
The same ideas that jam the machine, however, also dislodge
the letters that were waiting to be delivered, and they go off
like so many three-minute eggs, off white, soft, precise

enough to answer the same damn question that called up
those ideas in the first place. There is a mild swivel
about the day, a forest of cramps backlogged in an interruption.
There is, in fact, very little to be done, and even less
time in which to do it, as the diving evenings draw near.

At one end of an area, it's foggy and cool, with a hint
of sadness in the minds scattered about the pale, quiescent
avenues, while at the other end the sun, great author
of an engrossing, superlative pulp, sears the grass in trapezoidal
patches, bakes metal to a crisp, and wears soap operas down

in the health clubs instead of barely thinking. Aghast
is how the intervening country pays its due. The wealth
towers over the examples. Such needless display compounds
the already laughing matter with stays, pins, hardhats, joints,
and bricks, a mild form of nuance reversed into a bent, counter-
    punching

ardor that leans and will not go away, even when daunted
or put up to ripen in an unassuming, persnickety obsolescence.
Much later, having survived the near miss, not to mention the prosaic
slide presentation, the acolyte reaches home full of surprises
not so much to others as to himself, embarrassments such as giving

the steak to the cats, ranting over a limp, being a bear
in a rest area, impossibly, trashing the scene. He follows
the sex pixels. He follows, and it follows, in his career.
That is the straight map. Verbatim. Heaven hasn't the time
to refute it. String these marbles far from the blasting

lamps, the power has hold, and only old caverns resound
in a constant, the bought, coherent simple. Why not?
Let them drink clear water. The rain is in the air but never
comes down in summer, only heightens the air with a long
glance, perfect for spotting the drops in barometric pressure.

The music was being recorded so he didn't need to listen.
Full measure of bathing days reclined against the will.
He held in his hands the print of a former time. The sun
flickered through tense, a wayward strain to be anything like
the same. The fields were wide, but he cottoned to them.

Time can start again now. Instead of all these words
and no place to go. Only now does it help to have a plan
so that you know what you are supposed to do next
more or less. Things change from year to year but the sky
changes from day to day and stays the same from year

to year as far as we know. One wave comes after another.
Each is different, so they're unpredictable, real,
unique events, but at the same time there is a very
reassuring sense of security in the constancy of their assault
as if from an infinite energy source, in human terms, like the sun.

Like a volcanic eruption that releases tensions built up over
eons inside the earth and wreaks havoc in the daily lives
of fish and men, coughing slough and ash across the sun
in an awful revision of all that has come before, so an
interruption in the text, straight from the realm of reality,

where visions and versions clash by the light of a windward
moon and relations break down into fits and sobs and
defensive maneuvers aimed at gaining a toehold on history,
must, by the rules of this separation, be elided, folded
back into the continuance, a kind of stay of judgment

enabling a reader, later, only the vaguest clue that the
whole convulsive, withering, strident, referential mass didn't
spring into being in just the same rhythmic, variable
sittings as that later architect, you, reader, convened
to see what was up in a day. The interruption that is

places bets against the interruption that isn't. One
should always think and say that being is, but at times
the wind comes heavily down upon the racket. That noise
made retrospectively down the street signs its name in
chance, the wayward, confluent stamina it takes

to hold a job. In place, the time is only an instance
the parcel of land addressed as we. Parallel that back
to radio segments lost in a clamor of bricks. It takes
a unit to know the rules. Cane hobbles weep, the we
in an altered you subscribes to time. I've said everything

we hoped or planned in terms only they would understand.
Metering lights. Quality fools breathe style on the sore
points. I wouldn't want to have that camerooned.
An exquisite sensibility is worse than a row of cans,
useless as fame without money, a tidy, clinging kind

of self-satisfaction. Give me piles of used appliances
drenched in the crib. The noise of my earlier paradigms salutes
my need to know. There's a roll bar on the toll road, a song
breaks into the house, finishing off the last of it. You have odds
but the elegant works have an ache for all I know, being held

down by my otherwise perfectly assumable dental mortgage.
It is neither weight nor weightlessness that defines our host
but a continual referring back, a conversion of flux
to facticity, that language we thought you might find unsuited.
A calendar dotted with tire irons just floated a loan.

Newspaper articles, fancy dress, articles of war
and of law, these tones are merely parts of speech
in a syntax whose nouns are the times we set to sea
or made iced tea, filed insurance claims, or sat
on the porch feeling nice. The or a breeze ruffles the sheets

pinned to the line. They move over into it. The sun
carefully fills out a form, leaving the address blank.
Nowhere about this natural world is human drama, only
the integuments of the soil, washed out, splattered
into thin air, a combustion deprived of sound.

Snowshoe Thompson just went by. Chicago's Boso
with a big piece of turf in his helmet holds the ball
aloft. Boulders dot the embarrassment, dead trees
lie cracked and broken over the back pages, torrents
thrive on an orderly morning toilet. John C. Fremont didn't

write this. The fishing party collapsed on the point
of completing its catch—it hadn't wanted to end
things that way, but there you were. In any case, by breathing
we would certainly hand in our résumé on time, and it was only
a little way to the footbridge we had been told about

more than once. Then wetting our fingers at the breakwater,
we figured white would be ok for the exterior, clipping
our heads to the garbage cans made out of plastic. It was a pleasure
being left for dead, because no one would ever again tell us
we had to be somewhere. Instead we would always remember

the unfinished portrait of George Washington hanging in the front
of the classroom. A chimney stands where blackened
rubble covers the ground, an end to fear, where before
a sense of what might happen poisoned the neck and back
as viewers craned to see, as clear as mud, the ridge burn.

Wan rain, the slamming of blankets, then clarity
as stars stood straight up above the dampness. Way west
of this characteristic a movie was being made, waving glimpses
in the anterior cruciate night. Stars had gathered, the paper
come. A western woman took it in. Good morning to all you witches,

ghosts, hobgoblins, and especially all you skulls. Nothing is
     "instead of"
anything else — everything is itself, separate. That's not why
so much time passes while I don't write these words, words
that only serve to elide the Gargantuan truth of detail
waiting in the wings of a prayer, prayer that is this life, words

expressing our paucity or excessive force, one, an echo of that
voice I'd thought to hear then all but gave back, seemingly,
into the ground. Players, teams, Lithuanians, why should I
like anything? The legal staffing of batches wrenches
the sound you rub up against, making your friend come clean.

Doing things slowly, deliberately, takes up the better part
of the morning, one year. The work that is slowed, ongoing,
stays a mass of crystal with its slime. An incremental burgeon:
chained to a wall for five years, then: "We apologize for capturing
     you.
We see now that holding hostages serves no useful purpose."
     Released.

I'd thought to say something else, then bivouacked
and charted the rest in gold. My pulses were only
going to repeat themselves anyway, up to a point, as part
of the synoptic breadth. Land rays channeled to tunes,
a birthing, crested aromatic, semblance included. Tossed

a ball or something with some guys. There is no 'place'
for women in these networks; the door to the apartment house
is left half opened. Everybody needs to have some kind
of a help desk. These things don't run by themselves,
quite the opposite. All right. I've got four boxes

and I'm going to walk through each one. 1. Make
hard cuts to the opposite block. 2. Always jumpstop
to receive a pass. 3. Execute the required move and score
quickly. 4. Rebound and throw a hard outlet to the wing.
Squeak squeak sound of rubber soles on varnished pine.

As if the abstracted sense impression were a kind of bottom line.
Are these miracles science or are they just marketing ploys?
A whole rote sequence is packed into battery color.
The thickness of days, a clip art, subsidy, parental care,
and all that lucky time crowd into view. It's standing

room only in the bleached-out segments bearing little or no
resemblance but bringing chills to the table, as leaves
are used to make a lithograph. Perhaps I can help you,
but then again. . . . How much goes by in a minute, how
little in years! The clamoring, roseate substance of which

a day is made straddles the intervals, calm in a winter factory.
It falters like a headache under aspirin. After meditation,
cut a finger slicing bread or quarrel with someone you love.
The accompanying psychic shock will jar you out
from the docking station to which you have become hopelessly

affixed. Day rents space in a word. My watch
is going south. Honey is sugar; avoid it. The object
is replaced by a panoramic: "The World of Objects."
I don't *object* to that, it's just that. . . . Regional
differences pack the house. There is no mass experience

only that of individual beings. The mass is a facade.
White sugar all over the freeway. Behind the palisades
a bumpkin Dionysianism has set it. The illusion of being
kept up-to-date fades as you stand before the black painting.
You have to wait for your own retinal imagery to disappear

before you can see into it, the luminous mix of reds,
greens, blues, and blacks forming crosses, H's, and squares:
all black. It is a discipline to see. No sight but that
which uses art. The far station a mix, the landing
pads coherent in a further study. I wouldn't put it past

the answering impulse to swear up and down on a stack
and cast aspersions up like smack, a piece of man that works
and presses the button in time to topple the credenza. In case
there's no floor, the pathway leads to a mention, the particles
pile up into a body, rested but still slightly sore in the hip.

Morning, and a surround of nations stymies you. It sounded
ok in your head, but when you say it it sounds dumb. Wood
duck stamps for your bills and a no-parking space labeled LOADING
DUCK: before and after lunchtime treats on the second-to-last
day of not just any year, a line through these points points up.

Your excessive response is much appreciated in the quiet canyons
an undifferentiated economic impasse makes manifest, just
above the airline industry, several levels below Kansas City,
Missouri. I dance from pixilated candy that you have picked up
on the colorized situation to our left, where reality seems

to be running out of ink. Freud's Taos stands in for
the phrase. If something very important is being repressed or
denied, home values will soar. People in the late 40s, early 50s
in places like Carmel, Santa Monica, Cambridge, Greenwich
    Village, and Majorca
de Palma will gyrate to what you said. It will take a certain type

of person to piece together these bones. They form an instrument,
but I have taken the precaution of removing it from their sight.
The problems are not insoluble, but each solution seems
to present a new problem, so that one's work is never done.
Typing HELP followed by the name of a command displays help

for that command. Explaining how to get through a pick,
I believe. Triads are powerful crime groups with roots
in ancient China. *Rouge et noir* is a game in which
rows of cards are dealt and players may bet on which row
will have a count nearer 31 or on the color of the cards.

Does every game have as its object to win? I don't think so.
Home rhymes part fast. Stitch it here, along the grain. An
emptying out of old rules spreads the attention all
over, prepositional to a fault, as well as nowhere, that non-
location so precisely current as to limit every step of the cliché.

I would like to summon a few platitudes as we speed
across the plateau: something there is about the first-person plural
that does not love us as well as we believe we know. The middle
    part
of anything gets lost in a forest of beginnings and ends
which meet periodically, only having extension by virtue of veering
    off

into absentia. Bank, Ron, ball, Bowl. An extension
cord, a VCR, an antenna, and eight articles crammed
for an exam. Whole earth. Half sky. Wing nut. Dress lunch.
And in sleep, laid out beneath a police grid, dodging sex
dreams and trips to the PX, lost in a pulse, the same one

that ached in Uncle John's band, there, compliments of California
Casualty, the wayward instance flees, racked by theory,
fluorescent in haste, looking at five years, as it undoes its
splendor in advance of the road, cataloging a split in the nasty
ventilated cosmology recently employed on a part-time basis.

Yesterday I slipped out of the groove, and today had a good
deal of trouble getting back in. It was as if I was on the outside
looking in. But at the end of the day, the paper hit the front
steps the same way it always did, or would have anyway.
I don't conclude anything from this, on the contrary,

it doesn't seem to help much at all. The moot wings
of political roughage tear away, and we can see who's lying
on the fork in the road, throwing money up in the air like words
and endearing himself to no one in particular, a crude, vagrant
saunterer in correspondence with the stars, although their order

has never been more irresolute, because a hash mark has suddenly
planted itself between the earnings of an enervated public
and the only reason to come out here in the first place:
to shoot turkeys! Birds like turkeys and eagles are used
as metaphors for winners and losers in an attitude of mind

as American as apples to oranges, I mean, you can't really compare
what's lost to what's been happily gained then can you? It's
wise to be hopeful, grateful, and thoughtful, though not always
    possible.
Up? Down? Up down? What mood have you designated
to plot the morning shade? This is what you were

trying to tell them, that it had become impossible for you
to simply be one person. So that whereas the other focused
almost obsessively on a narrow range of social phenomena,
    attacking
it again and again from various angles in a broken, idiosyncratic
syntax, you enveloped all manner of disparate evidence

in a kind of emotional who-got-what-report, input,
processed, and published under the congenially rippling
banner of a commercially historicized rhetoric. Tough
totals. The anger flashed from pan to pan. Then a zoom
would be in order. I'll roil before two bits dent insight.

You have to gape at a flock like that, all birds pale
before the evening whirl. Going back over it in the second
half of life, you know barely more than the first time —
only to recognize it, the impulse pointing south, or west.
An aggregation of fragments, this life represents an opportunity to
    sit down

behind closed doors in a quiet room and concentrate on one thing:
House of Wrecks. A novel idea is what I just saw on the freeway
and how it works into my current thought stream, barely and with
    the edges
still visible if removed at some distance, say, a furlong. For as long as
this cautious adumbration hulks over the development cycle,
    research will have

to be speeded up, although we have no funds to spare for it or even
    to speak of.
And speaking of wrecks that speed into view for the first time,
what characteristic, when slapped with a fine spray, matches our
    synthetic
order in half the splendor? A plot to correspond with haste?
No, I don't think you mean that. It's just something

you put together in a moment off. An otherwise endless tunnel
of thought breaks out into the open at the written word, finite,
particular, breakneck, given to common usage, bright with age.
The wind is yea long. Our life continues without our knowledge
under everything of which we are most haltingly aware. The news

is last on our list. The taste of all that is missing most flagrantly
catches our style. Habits converge, and a lampstand totters
in the swirl an eddy rudders under time. Run the numbers once
again and you'll find a split infinite call, a conglomerated put,
and a wholesome diffidence in the face of world capital, when only

yesterday your best bet seemed to be to construct a light vessel
and pour yourself into the reading, alight with what to do
about the alarming mass of billing currently accruing but wise
to the off chance a senior analyst might show up to sort it
all out. Now the answer is up for grabs, not that the question has

exactly been put forward, it's more like a bemused look on
the furrowed collective brow of a beta test group, or an illness we
    read about
and immediately begin to imagine we have, or a flowering tree
    whose name,
if only we could remember it, would break open that awful aphasia
from which we have been suffering ever since, every since what?

Our birth? Or a simple metaphor, if metaphors can be said
to be simple, that would explain our position, speeding effortlessly
two inches above the glass, and not break into a million pieces
when held up to the light of philological scrutiny, a history
best left open for another time. The garden is covered

with a rich, fine carpet of spray. The ocean must be nearby.
A man born in the middle of a vast continent marries a woman
born on the coast of a small island. Their son, your correspondent,
born near a lake in the middle of the vast continent, situates
on the far edge, internalizes the vast distances the land mass
    manufactures,

rolls down the window on the tides, and, after a protracted youth,
    rolls up
his sleeves and settles down to business, doing detail work on
    contemporary
reversible conveyances. Behind an able man there are always other
    vegetable men.
In America today, the mainstream has dwindled to a pathetic
strand of calcified imagery holding the mind in thrall, and the
    margins are fat

with unlikeliness. Weeks go by between sentences, is that what's
    new
about them? Remember that variety is an important characteristic
of the power aisle. Include combinations of large and small items.
Make sure the signage faces the front entrance. Avoid randomly
    placed
stacks or displays. Line everything up in neat, even rows. These
    cautionary

trails have been beaten into the bush, and we follow them, not because
    we believe them to be leading anywhere in particular but because they offer
paths of least resistance into the interior, which generally turns out to be
someone else's exterior, but that's another story, stopping only to pick
the burrs from our socks. At rude angles with the way with words

the next blurt may be your own. There will, at all, be no surcease.
Into every other particular segment is injected a lifetime supply
of space, feeling tone rounding the character bends, false
witness creating a havoc of secular miles. Rage and shame enjoy
charter member status in the dormer pantheon we wear on our

way to work. It's a happy tab and a brisk summer tantalization
to which we have pulled ourselves up like zinc, and miles to go
before I wake. If I have taste, it is only for stuns. A story
line is a jail of bedposts. I have been meaning to write in poetry of its
own necessity: an opening. In our configuration centers, we can
    configure

a thousand kits per day. Line up and be counted I always say.
Five words after those words, we find the word "words." This
is a statement of surplus value. Any value implies a surplus.
    All hands
direct. These doors, torn from the jaws of time management,
open to porous copy on a litmus roll. See how vast and wide

the world is! Countless universes, known and unknown,
    step through
your minute concern. Why do you put on your seven-piece body
    at the sound
of the pound sign? Because Great Action, herself, appears, to hasten
you on your way. How long will it be before another entry graces
this gate? I cannot say, but stay up high and lean into the querulous
    light

the morning stars propose, bent on recognition, thriving on a tiff,
dug into alternate means, fledgling, where a band convenes a sound,
color-coded, reimbursable, just, festooned, and slick. I got a
    long-term
disability brochure today; that's about it. Moon resident in pink
    clouds
jet moves below overhead, you peel back the light on little kids
    on the street,

their sound I mean. That torch of hers. I started walking across the
    star-spangled
war-chest drayage under night's flip visage, not interested in
    anything I might
find, just out for a stroll, minding my own business really, though if
    the truth
were told I had none, for it was with no particular purpose that I set
    out, other
than the hygienic, wholly negative one of clearing the decks, so to
    speak.

What's different? The stars are gone. Day lies pitched like a hammer
in its cradle. Already the substitutions have begun. New York's
been going down since '88 and San Francisco has been rising.
Rain banks off rooftop water tanks, fog pillows on a dry bay.
To be a risk manager in a party dress, what's better than that?

What's happening? The line of roles stacks up to be a complete
    bypass,
a way around the main event, slipshod if at all extent, humus
black, flung attributes in the net of all seeing. I've got houses
in my lobes and they're all open, doors and windows spread
    to the four
winds. My foot is nailed to a shrine incineration. "Guess who's
    coming

to dinner." "A ghost." Having outlived body and mind the raging
spirit yanks a bulletin board from the wall, speaks in the night,
softly, incomprehensibly, no tape machine, no phone, three or four
hundred dollars extra to smoke on a sailing expedition with my
boss's boss's boss, whose home, burning in the hills, he'll never

see again. A squad broke into the RCA buildings, abandoned
and sealed up for two generations. They went down into the cellar
    arcades,
crumbling museums of the retail stores of centuries past. They
    located
the ancient elevator shafts and dropped through them into the
    subcellars
filled with electric installations, heat plants and refrigeration
    systems.

They went down into the sump cellars, waist deep in water from
    streams
of prehistoric Manhattan Island, streams that still flowed beneath
    the streets
that covered them. The sense of a city is war. The exhilaration
    mounts
in cooling plants in the outlying areas, a chorus to solo monotone
invoice tracking, a budget aside in a maximum battery

hairpin, resisting historic aphasia for horizontal reasons
if only from the legs on up. I guess the syntax that prepares
these lies lies open to any of us; we fill it with our various personal
chambers of horror, fitted out to wreck our sleep, images flat
against the rippling rhythm in defense of which we step out

of line, curve around back of the convalescent hospital, pick up
broken glass in one hand and check out every brick with the other,
secretly laughing on account of the compulsory overtime. If it
seems a random, solitary course, it is nonetheless one we share
who have nothing but the space under our feet, the salt

in our wounds, the baffling whispers from out in a bright hall,
and the miraculous streams of signals to wake us in time
for the workday. I have a feeling that no amount of preparation,
no matter how thorough, will be adequate to the moment, wherein
everything takes place. And yet it does not exist, except in

anticipation or retrospect. Thus meditations on time must end
in paradox, followed by taking the conversation off line. It is the
    brilliant
shortcoming of words to be inadequate, in the ultimate, to any
    subject,
and their savage grace to always be able to change it.
Life goes on, we always say, but does it? And so what if it does?

I won't be mollified by a panacea, er, a placebo, I'll sue the bejesus
out of the file server, I'm not complaining but I will be damned
and fry in hell before I totally accept this, this completely
    unacceptable
situation. The discharge in such a system is colorless. It empties
itself and the person goes on intermittently, deflecting annual
    epithets

rather than placing too much emphasis on particular nouns.
That's when I cram down my business-as-usual hat. But
the cost of goods sold must be factored into the equestrian
rattling the air with sword and shield. A sound or ache
is a framing device. In the foreground, pain. Inside the frame,

freedom. The fact is, and it's unfortunate, that before one has
had a chance to fully understand the situation, one dies.
The only conclusion I can draw from this is that one must act
on incomplete information. A certain level of attainment must be
    eschewed
in favor of cursory fact-checking and a quick trip to the loop

to pick up socks. Mine were knocked off by your insistent,
    paradigmatic
pulse, the life of style aflame in an extra inning, the wages garnered,
the heating lamps tilted back, all manner of what-have-you
    spattered and
crossed. And there, if I can just take this phone call, you have it,
    and it's
worth something, but only briefly. You'd do best to plow it back in.

Any such summing up is followed by a wide trough, like the silence
that follows responses to questions provoked by the posting of year-
    end results.
There is a dip in the blather quotient, a period of days during which
attention, although not unreflective, fails to nail itself down
    scriptwise
whether because it is simply too diverted by the ongoing rush of
    detail posing

as daily life or due to a kind of digital reticence, an unwillingness
    to sit
down, open the notebook, and begin, clueless as to what might
    transpire
there on the page containing the marks of already eclipsed
    sensations,
whether mental or rotten, curious, half-hearted or gut. If we do not
    write
it is because we are out there selling, pounding the roads, renting

cabins by torrential mountain streams that carry us off in our sleep
while we attend sleep school, unaware of the coincidence. Comedic
errands tug us across the changes. We are not ready to borrow
    another motor
until the music changes. Then the music ended and we were treated
    to the
clear rainwater sound. It had been what he had imagined the world

to be, streets, people in cars, windows, what others would later call
the common things of daily life, as opposed to what, metaphysics?
That was the first sentence of a work called "Sadness." But it had
    actually
been hammered out in glee, the type smacking the flat-skinned page
    in time
whose fluid beginnings housed torched chords in the rock hole wax
    in shifts

et cetera et cetera until there weren't any letters left, and the plane
    sound
echoed in his head at night. As if to register common nouns might
form a shape of empty time, freshening the scene, before becoming
instantly old again. Then lakes, masses, grains, delays, salvage
    yards,
and rotaries appeared in the forms of words. With realization,
    all things

are one family; with realization, all things are disconnected. The separateness
of the fingers supports connectivity solutions, interoperability, and a host
of client servers, all technical in their important, temporal appurtenances
but of little impact compared to a single wave. From the selling price you must
subtract the cost of goods sold to derive the gross margin. From the gross margin

you must subtract occupancy cost; sales, general, and administrative costs;
and any other costs of doing business to derive net profit. We live on
the margin. The gross domestic product is poetry. Otherwise, it's fucking.
Looking out the window is incremental business. Reading from books and games
on the floor represent growth, and at length there is tenderness, understanding.

I like that dancing in the kitchen. It's the joy of it coming off
the floor. Trading is heavy on a volume of one hundred million
shares, according to radio eastbound 580 at High, and I recognize
that most of it's wasted on me but I hope you agree there's pleasure
in the exchange, box-step for theory for light, shaken nightly into

the human yard. Ropes, days, hammers, spikes, troughs, wars,
and bulletin boards of scraps of paper stuck to concrete kiosks in
muddy markets mark the way, an array in aggregate, a popular
contrivance at last. And that's not the half of it. Between what
goes in—unutterable instants turning the neck to rubber — and
    what comes

out — endless lists, taxonomies fraught with hype, latex covers that
    bulge
and stretch to contain, speaking peoples alive in the hood — there is
    a margin
of error, a float, a delta or difference, exceeding all limits by the
    sound of it.
Separations in space, yeah, you got an alternator all right, right
here in your up-to-the-minute breath supply, oh host. We are guests

on this planet for such a short time it would seem, and yet one
contains multitudes, mirrored universes receding into the ten
    directions,
loss leaders sparking close-out sales amid frenetic retail traffic, west
counterpoised against night, day in and half out of place, all well
defined at a moment of simple composure, as you turn back to the
    well.

July 1991–December 1992

Ice Cubes II

■

open
window
put
air

conditioner
on
words
it

doesn't
really
matter
which

ones
hanging
by
them

on
the
lip
of

existence
let's
just
relax

and
finish
our
wine

■

being
with
fire
being

with
water
being
with

trees
standing
still
for

long
periods
of
time

■

a
neutrino
would
be

extremely
lucky
to
hit

anything
while
passing
through

an
atom
scientists
say

■

we
at
First
National

have
you
by
the

balls
I
remember
Evan

saying
in
New
Haven

■

there
are
no
people

in
the
centers
of

the
cities
at
night

only
a
few
conventioneers

and
tourists
drinking
quietly

■

work
chop
fades
out

under
the
windward
sun

parallax
blade
needle
wave

who
owns
the
sky

god
who
owns
the

earth
the
king
who

owns
the
ocean
we

do
said
the
girl

■

why
is
a
woodnymph

a
good
character
to

have
the
words
have

to
come
from
somewhere

■

it's
sometimes
worthwhile
to

have
one's
subjectivity
examined

■

you
don't
subscribe
to

the
dream
channel
but

you
get
it
anyway

■

there
is
a
dead

space
in
time
that

is
known
as
waiting

but
is
unknown
as

intelligent
life
on
Mars

you
have
to
go

outside
your
mere
expectation

you
must
be
warrior

■

the
avant-garde
is
our

home
away
from
home

■

Thursday
or
Friday
noon

looks
good
for
hoops

let
me
know
if

you
can
make
it

■

bone
supports
flesh
but

what
supports
bone
animation

conspiracy
de
la
soul

■

a
grain
of
salt

is
what
we
take

all
research
findings
with

■

glut
of
this
world

I
have
imposed
sanctions

by
having
my
cable

removed
for
the
duration

■

single
tack
pointed
up

chunk
of
coral
weird

bent
stick
red
rock

Hotel
Sovetskaya
lobby
pass

annotated
topography
a
bottle

of
pills
I
don't

have
to
take
anymore

■

all
mind
is
available

only
after
hours
in

light
of
the
sun

■

we're
always
looking
for

it
but
this
is

it
it's
very
disappointing

■

I'd
like
to
have

one
of
those
lung

clocks
to
measure
the

rhythm
of
life
against

what
do
you
say

nothing
hurts
to
say

■

the
camera
changes
everything

that
passes
before
it

■

lines
cascading
down
years

place
coffee
on
glass

mustache
feathers
stomach
muscles

wry
grin
in
passing

■

having
too
much
and

too
little
to
do

with
anything
the
crackling

hysteria
of
the
moment

intervenes
on
our
behalf

■

item
it
is
still

raining
outside
item
my

foot
is
not
sore

item
we
are
part

of
an
ongoing
concern

this
kind
of
thing

happens
all
the
time

■

breath
goes
in
and

out
heart
pumps
blood

to
brain
life
spills

over
into
night
streets

■

time
to
step
outside

the
normal
course
of

events
take
a
walk

around
the
block
the

block
is
huge
the

universe
must
be
expanding

■

we
are
no
longer

in
possession
of
the

Omaha
Steak
Flyer
a

lurid
four-color
depiction
of

various
cuts
of
meat

■

I
have
the
sense

that
history
is
chewing

us
up
and
swallowing

■

a
light
breeze
another

day
a
deep
breath

a
heart
beat
is

a
unit
of
measure

like
an
ice
cube

■

the
current
year
will

bring
you
much
happiness

I
can
believe
it

■

birds
above
transmission
shop

on
South
Van
Ness

■

sleep
deprivation
creates
a

sense
of
being
visited

by
someone
or
something

but
not
being
home

■

THOUGHT
contains
non-contiguous
blocks

■

I
don't
know
what

weapon
it
is
that

once
outside
your
doors

will
help
my
girlfriend

give
her
best
performance

■

wind
knocks
paper
cup

off
edge
of
ledge

it
bounces
and
rolls

in
a
wide
arc

scudding
against
the
concrete

■

dreams
seduce
memories
snag

leaves
tremble
water
collects

in
beads
on
leaves

■

I
find
my
words

have
outlived
their
own

meaning
which
is
vanity

but
do
walk
standing

out
against
summer
air

■

love
oh
love
oh

careless
the
tea
kettle

played
a
minor
seventh

July 1991–August 1992